FOULSHAM'S "NEW" POPULAR HANDBOOKS

TOASTS
AND
SPEECHES

HOW TO PREPARE
AND DELIVER THEM

BY

CHARLES R. CECIL
EDITOR OF "THE POPULAR RECITER,"
AUTHOR OF "THE BUSINESS LETTER-WRITER," "AN A.B.C. OF GRAMMAR," ETC.

REVISED EDITION
1949

LONDON
W. FOULSHAM & CO., LTD.
NEW YORK   TORONTO   CAPE TOWN   SYDNEY

MADE IN GREAT BRITAIN
BY TONBRIDGE PRINTERS LIMITED
PEACH HALL WORKS, TONBRIDGE, KENT
COPYRIGHT: W. FOULSHAM & CO. LTD

TO

THE INSTRUCTOR WHO LAUNCHED
ME ON THE " FIRST SOLO "

PREFACE

THIS little book is the result of an endeavour to provide genuine instruction and guidance for the individual who finds difficulty in expressing himself publicly, or who is but a beginner in the art of public speaking. The writer has been struck by the falsity of a number of booklets on the market at present which purport to demonstrate how audiences composed of royalty, nobility, and statesmen should be addressed. Obviously, it is absurd to suppose that those called upon to carry out such duties would require the aid of productions of this kind. Therefore there will be nothing within these covers commencing " Your Highness," " My Lord Bishop," etc.

The following chapters have been written expressly for the average man, who may be called upon to make a speech at ordinary social functions, at his trade union or association meetings, or at a debating club or political gathering. The writer's aim throughout has been, not to provide ready-made speeches for every possible occasion, but to show how the thing is done, and to give a few simple examples suitable as first efforts. In addition, some common faults of speech have been pointed out, and a hint or two given as to their eradication.

The contents has been arranged so that the reader may take up any particular branch of the subject wherein he is interested—perhaps " After-Dinner Speaking," perhaps the " Duties of a Chairman " ; but it is urged that the book be read as a whole, and due regard given to the first principles embodied in Chapters I., II., and III.

CHARLES R. CECIL

CONTENTS

PART I

HOW TO BECOME A GOOD PUBLIC SPEAKER

PART II

MODEL SPEECHES AND USEFUL MATERIAL
FOR SPEAKERS

CONTENTS

TOASTS AND SPEECHES

PART I

HOW TO BECOME A GOOD PUBLIC SPEAKER

CHAPTER I

THE FUNDAMENTALS OF CORRECT SPEECH

TWENTY years ago the average man had rare occasion and little inclination to make anything resembling what is called "a speech." Nowadays, however, consequent upon the growth of trade union organisations, the growing popularity of debating clubs and the like, and the widespread interest taken in public affairs, the desire to be able to express himself comes to every man. He realises that socially, in business—in every sphere of his activities. in fact—a good speaking voice and a command of good English form a valuable, almost indispensable, asset. Long-standing bad habits of speech, and, above all, that species of nervousness—akin to what is known as " stage fright "—which assails us all in our initial endeavours to address an audience, may seem almost impossible to overcome ; but study of the right use of the vocal organs, and of the science of articulation, inflexion, modulation, and pitch, will enable the poorest speaker to become, if not an orator, at least a good conversationalist. Time spent in this study can never be considered as wasted ; clear, intelligible, expressive utterance of what you have to say never fails to exert an influence in your favour when those with whom you come in contact are forming their judgment of you.

Oratory is an art ; speech, of whatever nature, is always a science—and it must, primarily, be studied as such. The overcoming of the beginner's nervousness referred to above is, obviously, largely a question of screwing up sufficient courage to take, as it were, the first plunge. If, when you have decided to take the plunge, you are wise enough to make your speech a short one, and to choose for its subject a question wherein you have genuine convictions, you will find that, once having started, the desire to make clear your arguments will banish all your embarrassment.

The study of elocution will prove itself of value in enabling you to avoid many of those awkward lapses which ever seem to lie in wait for the unwary. Here it may be emphasised that few people realise the vital importance of correct breathing as a fundamental necessity to all good speaking, although its importance in regard to good singing is more generally understood.

The question of correct respiration is of such importance that we will consider it first, and in some detail. The vocal organs consist primarily of the lungs, the trachea or windpipe, and the larynx. The lungs, acting exactly as a bellows, force air through the trachea into the larynx, where the most delicate muscular mechanism, directed by the brain, forms (and controls as to key and intensity) the vocal sound. This sound is still further moulded in its passage through the mouth by the relative positions of the uvula, palates, tongue, teeth, and lips.

Inspiration should be frequent, and sentences should be so phrased that fresh breath may be taken before the actual necessity arises. To do all this, the rib muscles which regulate the action of the lungs must be under complete control, and for this the adoption of what is known as costal breathing is recommended.

There are three methods of breathing, known as clavicular, costal, and abdominal. The second method, undoubtedly the best, consists of what is aptly described as " throwing out the chest." There is considerable increase in the middle and lower diameters of the thorax, and the abdomen should be slightly concave. It has been proved mathematically that by far the greatest use of the capacity of the lungs can be made in this way, and it will be found that the regulation of the outgoing air is easier in this method than in any other.

Inhalation should be, as far as possible, through the nose ; but the point of paramount importance to be remembered is that the taking of a breath must be accomplished with absolute silence.

Let your diction be slow ; correct respiration will be easier, you will be more impressive, and you will have more time to think.

The student who understands the significance of correct breathing and resolves to pay some attention thereto should next turn his attention to those of the vocal organs, existing above the larynx, which mould the various sounds and form the *quality* or *timbre* of the voice. There are eighteen distinct vowel sounds in English, and the actual laryngeal sound for all of them is the same, the various shades of difference being made by the positions of those organs situated within the cavity of the mouth. Of these, the tongue, teeth, and lips are most worthy of attention.

Probably the commonest faults of English-speaking people are inadequate opening of the mouth and failure to use the teeth and lips sufficiently in articulating. It is by no means difficult to remedy these defects, and a little time and care expended in practising articulation will produce surprising results in regard to the speaker's " range," besides relieving his throat of a good deal of strain.

To correct faults in enunciation and articulation it is a good idea to practise speaking before a mirror, taking careful note of the position of the teeth and lips when making the various component sounds of a word. Needless to say, the words must be spoken very slowly ; and the exercise may be reasonably confined to words which you suspect yourself of clipping or slurring. At the same time, make it a habit to observe good speakers. All speech is acquired by imitation, and correct speech no less so than any other sort. But your study of a good speaker should not be confined to listening— watching his mouth will help you in imitating him as will nothing else.

In connection with mirror practice, the following table will be found useful, as giving some indication of the lines practice may take :

Sounds	Nature	Exercise
Ah, Oo, O A, E, and Aw	Vowel	Note varying shape of mouth and amount of teeth covered by lips.
I, Ou, and Ow Oi and Ai	Diphthongal (mixed vowels)	Note two rapid positions of tongue and mouth; and that $\quad$ I $\quad=$ Ah plus E $\quad$ Ow $=$ Ah ,, O $\quad$ Oi $\;=$ Aw ,, EE $\quad$ Ai $\;=$ A $\quad$,, E
P, B, M	Labial	Observe contact of lips, and nasal sound in M.
F, V	Labio-dental	Observe difference of position of lower lip in touching upper teeth.
J, D Th, Dh (as in wi*th*) S, Z, Sh, and Zh	Dental	Note position of tongue in relation to teeth.
Th, Sh, W L, N R (trilled)	Miscellaneous	Note protrusion of lips. Note position of tongue at back of upper teeth. Pay special attention to tongue.

Resonance, pitch, inflection, and modulation are subjects of which far more can be learnt from experience and study of good speakers than from textbooks.

Resonance may be defined, somewhat inefficiently, as that resounding quality of the voice resulting from the reverberation of the vocal sound in the cavities of the nose, mouth, and chest (the latter can be *felt* vibrating in the production of " chest " notes).

The question of pitch, too, is one of some difficulty ; the middle notes of the speaker's compass, as those obtaining most resonance from the chest, are the most useful to him ; and the lowest of the middle four is probably the best upon which to commence a speech.   Changes of key or pitch should, however, be effected in order to give variety of utterance ; and these should coincide with changes of subject.

That power of vocal expression depending on inflection and modulation is the hall-mark of the speaker of excellence, and it is only manifested when inspiration is coupled with the skill obtained by long study and experience.

The main points of this chapter may be with advantage recapitulated as injunctions to practise at every opportunity, to inhale silently and frequently ("throwing out" the chest), and to speak slowly, framing each word carefully and distinctly.

CHAPTER II

PRONUNCIATION, VOCABULARY, AND STYLE

REFINEMENT of speech is necessary to all who would become good public speakers.   And here it may be said that the possession of a brogue or accent such as that of an Irishman or Northerner should by no means be considered a defect ; for, given that a speaker uses good grammatical construction, and does not actually mispronounce words, his brogue not infrequently lends a distinct charm to his discourse.

The use of the aspirate, however, and the pronunciation of some of the more unfamiliar of our words are matters that require attention from almost everyone.   It is quite common to hear such expressions as "izzee" for "is he," and "he-oo" for "he who" ; these are the very natural results of rapid and slurred speech, and will disappear if a speaker will but remember to deliver each word separately and deliberately.   A far more irritating defect, and one much more difficult to eradicate, is the habit of misplacing the aspirate. In their desire not to omit it, some people tack the letter " h " on to almost every word beginning with a vowel. Since it is mainly the outcome of nervousness, this fault is more easy of correction after the speaker has gained some confidence from his initial attempts. He should practise by reading aloud very slowly some good selection of English prose (it is not necessary to inflict this on an audience) ; and thus, while acquiring command of the refractory aspirate, the musical rhythm and balance so necessary to the quality of good English, written or spoken, will be impressed upon him.

Misuse of the letter " h " is frequently the result of failure to observe a very useful rule regarding the pronunciation of the little word " the." Before a vowel the word " the " should be pronounced as " thee " ; before an " h " it should be pronounced as are the letters " th " in the word " leather." Many people invert this rule, and the result is such errors as " the hambition " and " the 'ouse."

Another common defect is the introduction of an " r " between a word which ends with a vowel and the following word which begins with a vowel—such as " the idear of," and " I sawr an engine," etc. This fault also can be corrected by slow speaking and reading practice.

A speaker should aim continually at the extension of his vocabulary. Nevertheless, in speech, the familiar word should always be given preference over the far-fetched, the short over the long, and the concise phrase over the circumlocution.

One still finds many people with extremely hazy ideas regarding the difference in meaning and pronunciation between such words as complaisant and complacent ; deprecate and depreciate ; palatial and palatal ; ascetic and æsthetic ; veracity and voracity ; allusion and illusion ; proscribe and prescribe ; mendacity and mendicity ; principle and principal ; perspicacity and perspicuity. These, and doubtless many others, will repay the looking up in a good pronouncing dictionary. You should make a habit to hunt up every word the pronunciation or meaning of which is doubtful to you, and to continue the practice with every new word you meet. By this means your vocabulary will be increased by far more than the number of words about which you actually consult your dictionary, since each new word will supply a clue to the meanings and pronunciations of several others.

Vocabulary may be increased by any kind of reading provided it is fairly extensive. The student will be well advised, however, to apply himself more particularly to the works of really good writers (of which there is an immense and varied supply in cheap editions), for from good literature so much of great value besides vocabulary is to be gained.

In acquiring that refinement and distinction of speech associated with the best education, much assistance may be gained by joining a debating club or similar society. You will be able to study closely the good and bad points of your fellow-members as speakers, and you will have the advantage of their probably candid criticism of yourself. In addition, the interchange of ideas will broaden your outlook and render you conversant with many new aspects of life.

Even in a small gathering of speakers you will find great diversity of style and manner of delivery. On the subject of gesture you will probably obtain considerable enlightenment. As a nation we English are extremely averse to anything in the nature of gesticulation ; and the question of how to stand and what to do with one's hands is a fairly big problem to all speakers at first.

Your actions, if any, must appear absolutely spontaneous and natural. By far the best plan is to indulge in no gestures except those which *are* absolutely spontaneous and natural. In other words, restrain yourself from making any illustrative movements with your hands and arms, endeavouring to get the desired emphasis by impressive diction. When you get warmed to your subject you will probably be unable to refrain from making some gestures to drive home your points ; and these, since they are quite spontaneous, will be effective.

When standing up to make a speech, assume a comfortable and easy attitude. Your hands, which may seem at first in the way, you should dispose of by clasping them behind you, resting them on a rail or chair-back, or putting them in your pockets—and leaving them there. (But remember, if you put them in your pockets, to avoid jingling your money ; such habits become exceedingly irritating to an audience.)

In order to be able to turn the more easily from side to side rest the weight of the body on one foot rather than on both. But do not sway from side to side continually. And do not fix your eyes upon the ground ; look at your audience, though not at any particular individual.

The value of the foregoing hints will probably be well illustrated by the speakers whom you will observe at a debating club. The marring effects of certain habits, of phraseology particularly, will also present themselves to you. You will notice that the use of hackneyed quotations and expressions is somewhat displeasing ; and the following may be taken as phrases to be avoided, or at most used once only, and for a particular reason : " To be or not to be ; " " the man in the street ; " " more honoured in the breach than in the observance ; " " the light fantastic toe ; " " the soft impeachment ; " " filthy lucre ; " " few and far between." There are many others, of course, equally threadbare.

If a quotation is to be used it is worth while to quote correctly. It is common to hear " Fresh fields and pastures new," the correct rendering of which is " Fresh *woods* and pastures new." Another instance is, "A little knowledge is a dangerous thing ; " correctly, the phrase runs, " A little *learning* is a dangerous thing."

Certain words, too, are very often wrongly used. For instance, the verbs " to lie " and " to lay " are confused in everyday speech to an extraordinary extent. It should be remembered that the verb " to lay " is transitive—that is, a person who lays must lay *something*, as a hen or a bricklayer does. To lay *down* is a physical impossibility.

Again, archaic and obsolete words have no merit in themselves, and are liable to strike a listener as an affectation. "Yclept," "whilom," "methinks," "behest," "peradventure" —to quote a few examples—are not in keeping with modern speech, and they are, moreover, open to misapprehension.

Care should be taken also to avoid finishing a sentence

with a preposition or other insignificant word. A professor of English is credited with having said that " a preposition is the one word which you must not end a sentence *with*," thus, perhaps unintentionally, doubly emphasising his point. Such a sentence has a weak, ragged, incomplete effect. " What subject are you speaking on ? " lacks the finished, rounded form of " On what subject are you speaking ? "

The question of the use of slang may occur here, and, whilst it would be too much to aver that slang should never be used, it must be pointed out that only in certain circumstances is it in any way effective or desirable. To some audiences, quite possibly, your arguments will be much more comprehensible and forcible if couched in the language which they themselves affect. Under such circumstances some slang may perhaps be permissible ; but it should be borne in mind that the English language, wielded properly, is capable of expressing practically any idea without becoming in any way obscure, and that slang is usually the outcome of a limited vocabulary. When speaking on sporting subjects, of course, sporting slang may be used, and cannot be objected to unless it is overworked. In any case, it is a good plan to use slang sparingly. This rule ensures that if, and when, resorted to, a slang expression becomes particularly trenchant.

Metaphor and allegory are adopted to picture an idea the more vividly. In all figurative speech the image chosen should be suited to the subject, and the metaphor must be consistent throughout. By this it is not meant to debar a speaker from using a succession of apt metaphors.

The use of Latin tags and foreign phrases cannot be commended. It is true that there are some abstractions that can be expressed only with difficulty in English, and for which it is often advantageous to employ a foreign idiom. But such expedients will but rarely assist you in making your meaning clear to an average audience ; and, generally, they will conclude you are airing your knowledge. And it is well to bear in mind that an effort to show off learning often results in an exposure of ignorance.

Your object as a speaker should be to say what you have to say so as to instruct or persuade your hearers ; and with this end in view, your keynote should be simplicity.

It is perhaps impossible to recapitulate this rather discursive chapter after the manner adopted in the preceding one ; but the student will profit if he keeps in mind the importance of (1) slow reading aloud as an aid to correct use of the aspirate ; (2) regular reference to a good dictionary as a means to extended vocabulary and correct pronunciation ; (3) intellectual conversation and reading as methods of broadening the mind ; and (4) simplicity of language and gesture as the foundation of effective style.

CHAPTER III

PREPARING A SPEECH

In your preliminary attempts at speech-making you may find that notes are more hindering than helpful. In overcoming your nervousness, short narratives and descriptions—spoken essays, in fact—will serve as the best exercises. From these you may progress to short criticisms of, or replies to, other persons' speeches. But at this stage the necessity for brief notes will make itself apparent ; and as soon as you feel confident enough to discuss a subject at some length, this preparation of the necessary notes must engage your attention.

In roughing out a speech there are several rules to be remembered. The point to be established must always be borne in mind, and every argument used should bear directly upon and lead rationally up to that point.

Digression of any kind must be rigidly excluded. Excursions into bypaths tend to distract the minds of your hearers, and possibly your own mind, from the main theme. They also use up time unprofitably. Every fresh fact or argument should proceed easily and logically from that preceding it ; and it is in enabling you to ensure this that notes are of greatest value.

It has been said that the best advice on making a speech is embodied in the injunction to " stand up, speak up, and shut up." And very truly, too, for there is a great deal more in the phrase than is at once apparent. To stand up physically you will have already learnt. But you have still to stand up to your subject, to deal with it fairly, squarely, and thoroughly. Speaking up, also, applies as much to the substance of your discourse as to the manner of its delivery ; you must ensure that your method of treatment is worthy of the subject you expound and the audience you address. And to shut up is not the easiest part of a speaker's task. Simply to dry up because your supply of ideas has run out will undo any good you may have achieved. Your various arguments have to be brought together and rounded off in a climax, which will leave your hearers with a clear-cut impression of unassailable logic arriving at an absolutely right conclusion. Having reached your culminating point, you should never on any pretext return to go over old ground.

The arrangement of your notes should conduce to all these desired excellences. A few ideas jotted down anyhow will be much more likely to confuse then to assist you. Care expended in preparing notes will help you in two ways. The preparation will serve practically as a rehearsal of the speech, fixing the ideas strongly in your brain ; the notes themselves, when referred to, will be immediately intelligible, and a real help.

Before proceeding, however, with the preparation of notes, a clear understanding of the essential component parts of a speech must be obtained. These parts may be regarded as being six in number, each following rationally from that preceding, all in direct relation to each other and the whole. They are as follows :

(1) General introduction of subject.
(2) Statement of the particular proposition which is to be expounded.
(3) The evidence in detail.
(4) The summary of evidence.
(5) Exposition of the conclusion logically to be drawn from such evidence.
(6) The appeal for support, or the " peroration."

Under these headings your notes may most conveniently be set down. Naturally, certain of the divisions are capable of further subdivision. Evidence in detail, for instance, may well have six divisions of its own, the number being mainly dependent on its bulk.

Let us suppose, for the purpose of a practical example, that you have to deliver a speech on " The Need for Prison Reform." Having acquired a fair knowledge of your subject, you come to the preparation of your notes.

First comes the question of how to open. Your introduction must be of a nature to arrest attention. Some topical or personal reference will generally achieve this end, and is the method very frequently adopted. In the present instance it will do very well.

Now, then, for the first note. Since the question is of prisons, recent police proceedings will supply a topical reference. Select a case that has received a fair amount of press comment, and under the first of the headings mentioned above, write down—

(1) John Smith, burglar. 3 years.

Having mentioned this case in opening your speech, you have to lead up to the subject of Prisons. On prisons few people have very definite ideas. You may bring this home to them by asking whether they have any idea where and to what John Smith is going. Very good ; write as a second note, under the same heading—

Where is he going ?

You will probably be able to enlarge on this, either by describing a personal visit to a prison or, failing that, by quoting from the report of a recent Parliamentary Committee. Here is a further note to make. Under your heading of General Introduction you have, then, this—

(1) John Smith, burglar. 3 years.
Where is he going ?
Personal visit (or Parliamentary Report).

Passing to heading (2) you have to set out your " argument " or the proposition you wish to prove. For this, bearing in mind that you wish to show that our prisons need reform, you had best give some reasons why as at present constituted they are wrong. You think, perhaps, that it is because they are out of date. Society's attitude to criminals has changed, but parallel changes in prison buildings and, to some extent, the system, have lagged behind. Most of our prisons were built before the idea of reformation and rehabilitation of prisoners was generally accepted ; and prison administration, while greatly improved, is still in need of reform. Under (2), then, write down—

> (2) Prisons need reform.
> Buildings no longer suitable.
> Administration needs modernisation.

With (3) we come to the presentation of the evidence you have acquired by reading up your subject, or in other ways. Its quantity will be governed by your time-limit to a certain extent ; but if the time allowed you is short, you should economise it by compressing details rather than by omitting them. Your notes of evidence may appear something like this :

> (3) Physical overcrowding.
> Poor hygiene and sanitation.
> More " open prisons " needed.
> Stultifying influence of unnecessary petty restrictions.
> Inadequate provision of useful employment.
> Lack of proper educational facilities.
> Insufficient classification and segregation of prisoners.
> Insufficient constructive reformatory work.

On each of these sub-headings you should be able to discourse for two minutes or more, forcing your hearers to realise what these things mean.

For the summary of this evidence it will merely be necessary to make a note thus—

> (4) Overcrowding and bad conditions.
> Repressive influences.
> Insufficient rehabilitation.

The logical conclusion of all the foregoing is that the system is out of date and fails to put into effect present-day ideas on the treatment of criminals. Make a simple note to the effect :

> (5) System out of date.
> Theory not put into practice.
> Vast improvement necessary.

Your peroration should have all the eloquence of which you

are capable ; and, as a keynote, you might jot down as a final aid—

> (6) Ignorance of the facts alone could permit the continuation of these conditions in a really progressive community !

As a whole, your notes will appear thus—

(1) *General Introduction*.
> John Smith, burglar. 3 years.
> Where is he going ?
> Personal visit (or Parliamentary Report).

(2) *Statement of Particular Proposition to be Expounded*.
> Prisons need reform.
> Buildings no longer suitable.
> Administration needs modernisation.

(3) *The Evidence in Detail*.
> Physical overcrowding.
> Poor hygiene and sanitation.
> More " open prisons " needed.
> Stultifying influence of unnecessary petty restrictions.
> Inadequate provision of useful employment.
> Lack of proper educational facilities.
> Insufficient classification and segregation of prisoners.
> Insufficient constructive reformatory work.

(4) *Summary of Evidence*.
> Overcrowding and bad conditions.
> Repressive influences.
> Insufficient rehabilitation.

(5) *Exposition of Logical Conclusion from Evidence*.
> System out of date.
> Theory not put into practice.
> Vast improvement necessary.

(6) *Peroration*.
> Ignorance of the facts alone could permit the continuation of these conditions in a really progressive community !

If your memory is good, or if you have had some little experience, the above could advantageously be cut down to—

(1) John Smith. Personal visit.
(2) Reform. Buildings unsuitable. Administration out of date.
(3) Overcrowding. Hygiene. " Open prisons." Restrictions. Employment. Education. Classification. Constructive work.
(4) Overcrowding. Repression. Rehabilitation.
(5) Out of date. Theory—practice. Reform.
(6) Ignorance—progressive community.

A beginner would be ill-advised, however, to attempt a

speech from notes cut down to this extent. The longer form is clearer, and if well spaced and arranged can hardly mislead him.

In part (2) of a speech it is usually necessary, besides stating your proposition, to define the terms used therein. In the example used this was not necessary; but had your subject been, say, " Flaws in Social Security," it would have been necessary to explain what you meant by " flaws " and by " social security." Omitting to define your terms will almost invariably ensure your being misunderstood.

The " peroration " is the appeal to the heart made after all possible has been done by appealing to reason. Speakers who do not possess the gift of rhetoric are best advised to close with a quiet request for a verdict on the evidence shown.

Before leaving the subject it must be admitted that some authorities advise that a beginner should write out the whole of his speech, commit it to memory, and have the whole of the manuscript with him for reference when his ordeal arrives. It is true that some of our most brilliant speakers have followed this practice; and it is also true that the most striking phrases of any speech are more often the result of deliberate preparation than of the inspiration of the moment. The practice is, nevertheless, not commended herein, as it so often leads to flat monotonous delivery, and to complete confusion in the event of the speaker " losing his place."

CHAPTER IV

AFTER-DINNER SPEAKING

THERE are doubtless many who, without wishing to deliver controversial speeches, feel that they would very much like to attain some proficiency in what is called " after-dinner speaking." For everyone who mixes with his fellows socially is bound at some time or other to be called upon for a speech ; and at every social gathering a few of the right words said in the right way go far indeed towards setting each individual at his ease, convinced he is in excellent company. Again, there may be others who, holding some office, such as secretary of a social or sporting club, find that the preparation and presentment of reports fills them with undue misgiving.

Correct enunciation, diction, and construction are, if possible, even more important in the non-controversial type of speech than in the type already dealt with ; therefore a beginner must first give attention to the principles already outlined.

The after-dinner speech is usually a preliminary to the proposal of a toast, or a response thereto. Consequently its essential qualities should be gracefulness and geniality. A humorous element, though not essential in all cases, is generally advantageous. Obviously, notes cannot be used, so that the student of this branch of the art of elocution must specialise, if he can, in extempore speaking. But—at first, at any rate—preparation of the whole speech beforehand is the best plan to adopt whenever it is possible. Initial efforts should be brief—just a few well-constructed phrases of appreciation. These will have much greater effect than a tedious string of disjointed remarks interspersed with many " um's " and " ah's." This fault requires considerable effort to eliminate. In after-dinner speaking it is very common, and detracts greatly from what might otherwise be neat, graceful delivery. Other faults are the use of too ponderous and laboured humour, and, perhaps most of all, repeated deliberate punning.

The proposition of what are called " loyal " toasts, such as " The King" and " The Royal Family," will be of course a more formal affair than the usual run of after-dinner speeches. So also will be the proposing of the health of certain personalities at formal banquets. But such duties are almost invariably assigned to old hands, so that a beginner will not go far wrong in making it his aim to be light and entertaining. Five minutes is probably the utmost time his speech should occupy ; but although short compared with expository speeches, it must have a concentrated excellence and a glitter that cannot be obtained usually by leaving anything to chance. Therefore, a toast or a response should be mapped out in advance, and subjected to much pruning and polishing.

It may so happen, however, that a speaker may find himself

anticipated ; a previous speaker, quite by accident, may use your choicest *bon mot* and render useless your carefully prepared address. Here the advantage of ready wit manifests itself. You will be practically forced to speak entirely extempore ; and if unable to cope with the situation, your best plan is to admit frankly that you have been anticipated, and to confine yourself to as few words as possible.

The planning of an after-dinner speech, then, should be on the following lines :

The subject of the toast should be eulogised with as much sincerity as possible. Select some of his qualities that you genuinely admire, calling the attention of your audience to them and advancing your reasons for admiration. Choose a suitable anecdote, if you can, to illustrate the theme of your discourse. Round off with an epigram of your own construction, or an apt quotation. Couch the whole speech in the choicest language of which you are capable, being careful that its tone suits the audience. Go over the whole two or three times, repolishing and cutting out anything superfluous.

But, you will say, what about that most difficult part, the opening ? The question has been left purposely to be dealt with separately. It is in framing a good opening sentence that one often experiences most difficulty. Well, then, on this point let it be understood that the best plan is to begin by saying what you really feel about the job that has been thrust upon you. Say whether you feel pleased, honoured, reluctant, unfitted, etc., as the case may be. Even if you stand up and blurt out, " I hate doing this," you will find that the general tendency will be to hail you as a unique wit rather than as a fool In the following pages will be found several ready-made speeches given at full length, together with several frameworks on which you may build up your own speeches for various occasions. The speeches given at full length should be regarded as models and indications of the lines you should follow rather than as actual speeches to be learnt by heart. But if you have an extremely low opinion of your own powers, you may, by reading them through (possibly combining parts of two or three), find something which, memorised, may serve your purpose.

Responding to a toast will be found, on the whole, easier

than proposing one. Brevity is expected, and if you do not feel confident you need do little beyond return thanks. If, however, you wish to " pad " your speech somewhat, you will find ideas are ready to hand in the remarks that the proposer of the toast has made. While he was making them, certain comments are bound to have occurred to you ; if he has raised a laugh, you should be able to raise another by a reference to some other aspect of his witticism. First efforts in after-dinner speaking may well take this form.

With regard to the other type of non-controversial speech—namely, the report or statement such as a secretary or treasurer has at certain intervals to submit to his committee—very little needs to be said. Undoubtedly the best plan is to prepare your report *in extenso*, and to read it out. Facts in detail, arranged briefly, and so as to be easily comprehensible, are what you will be expected to furnish. The arrangement of your facts should follow some definite order, either chronological or that of their relative importance. At the conclusion it is sometimes an advantage to add a few words illustrating, say, the total effect of all the things that have been done or left undone, or the comparison between the period dealt with and some previous period. Examples are given in Chapter IX.

CHAPTER V

THE DUTIES OF A CHAIRMAN

Upon the choice of a suitable individual as chairman the smooth running and success of a gathering largely depend. The most simple method of election is for one of those present to say, " I propose that Mr. So-and-So be appointed chairman," and for another person to second the proposal. If other names are proposed, a vote should be taken by a show of hands.

A chairman should be genial, tactful, preferably a fairly able speaker, and must possess some force of character. His position invests him with the authority to maintain order at the meeting, and he should be able to use his authority to ensure to every speaker a fair hearing without any unseemly interruption. At convivial gatherings the maintenance of an atmosphere of good-fellowship rests with the chairman ; and on such occasions he should be able to assert sufficient authority to prevent any unruliness or disturbance.

At a formal meeting, such as a committee meeting, the chairman's first duty is to state briefly for what purpose the meeting has been convened. He will then cause the minutes of the previous meeting to be read, and after this has been done, will ask someone to move " That the minutes be approved." If the motion is carried, he signs the minute-book. If any objections are raised, he sees that the necessary alterations are made before signing.

This having been done, he announces, clearly and concisely, the first subject for discussion, and calls upon the first speaker by name. If the meeting should be a political one, or if the proceedings are to take the form of a debate, he will introduce the chief speakers, each in his turn, always remembering to be brief. After the chief speaker or speakers have had their say, it is the chairman's duty to announce that the subject is open for discussion. Should two persons rise at once to speak, he should request one by name to proceed, and call upon the other as soon as the first sits down. If any speaker shows a tendency to wander from the point, to become personal, or to take up too much time, the chairman must call his attention to the subject under discussion and the fact that there is but a limited time for each speaker.

At the end of a discussion the chairman will put before the meeting the proposal or motion on which a vote is required, and will ascertain the votes for and against either by a show of hands or a division. He will then announce whether the motion is lost or carried, stating the majority. Should there be an equally divided vote, he may give his casting vote.

Any amendment to a motion which may be proposed must be voted upon before the motion itself. When the agenda of the meeting has been carried out the chairman will formally declare the meeting at an end.

At social gatherings the chairman's duties are somewhat different. At banquets and the like a vice-chairman is also appointed, who rules at the further end of the table, and relieves the chairman of some of his duties.

The chairman's chief duties are to propose the loyal toasts—
" The King," " The Royal Family," " The Services," etc.—and
the health of the guest of the evening if there be one.

If arrangements have not been already made, it devolves
upon the chairman to arrange the seating at dinner. Here,
again, great tact is essential in securing for each diner, as
far as possible, suitable neighbours. The guest of the evening,
of course, always has the place of honour to the right of the
Chair.

In proposing the loyal and special toasts it is customary for
the chairman to call upon the responders by name. Unless
royalty be present there is no response to the toast of " The
Royal Family." There is never any response to the toast of
" The King."

CHAPTER VI

SUGGESTIONS FOR THE FORMATION OF SPEAKERS' CLASSES, WITH RULES FOR THE FORMATION OF DEBATING CLUBS, ETC.

IT frequently happens that persons who have never spoken in
public are averse from joining established debating clubs,
although they are genuinely anxious to acquire experience in
speaking to an audience. For these, a small, more or less
informal, speakers' class is an excellent institution.

It needs but four or five such individuals to start a class,
but they must first enlist the sympathy and services of one
who has some ability in public speaking, and experience as a
chairman, if possible, to act as their teacher.

The teacher will act always as chairman, and will use his
tact and experience to assist the more nervous beginners. At
the first meetings he should give or read a short address on
the principles of good speaking. He should then call upon
each one present to speak for, say, two minutes on any subject.
Generally a request for some personal reminiscence elicits the
most ready response. Those whose nervousness is so great
that they cannot bring themselves to speak at all may be

given one or two short passages to read, paying special attention to articulation, etc. It has been the author's experience
that the most one can expect of some persons at the very first
is that they will stand up and say, with prompting, " Mr.
Chairman, Ladies and Gentlemen " ! This, exaggerated as it
may seem, need not be considered wholly as failure. For, at
least, the individual has been made to *stand up* and to say
something.

After each little speech or effort at correct reading, the
teacher should offer a few critical remarks. In this he should
adopt a courteous, perhaps fatherly, manner, being careful
always to give due prominence to any slight improvement he
can discern. At the second and two or three subsequent
meetings the members of the class should be confined more
and more to giving their opinions on controversial topics, the
same system of criticism being carried out. As a variation
other members of the small audience may be invited to offer
criticism.

At, say, the fourth or fifth meeting the chairman should
give a short address on the component parts of a speech and
the system of arranging notes, as outlined in Chapter III.,
presenting, if possible, each member with a copy of the six
headings under which his or her notes should be made. At
subsequent meetings speeches on subjects suggested by the
chairman or chosen by themselves should be prepared beforehand and delivered by the members in turn. The criticism
may now be made a little more severe, and the attention of
individuals directed to their own particular bad habits and
faults.

After a short time it will be found interesting to devote
about half the time of a meeting to prepared speeches, and
the remaining half to a short debate on some topic proposed
and decided upon by vote. After this stage the evolution of
the class into a debating circle pure and simple will be almost
inevitable ; and when, by general opinion, the need for the
criticising system is no longer felt, no time should be lost in
constituting, with the correct rules and officers, a proper
debating society.

A debating society should have the following officers :

    1. A President or Chairman.

2. Vice-President or Vice-Chairman (one or more).
3. A Secretary and Treasurer (or, if desired, these offices
   may be held by separate individuals).

A Committee should be formed of all the officers and at least
an equal number of members.

The President, or his " Vice," will take the chair at all
meetings ; his duties will be found outlined in Chapter V.

The Secretary has charge of all the society's correspondence,
is responsible that the minutes are entered up, and it is his
duty to arrange debates with other clubs, and to inform
members whenever meetings are to be held.

The Treasurer has charge of members' subscriptions, sees
that they are paid, and keeps the accounts of the society
generally. On him rests the responsibility of paying for the
premises in which meetings are held, if any such payment is
necessary.

The Committee select subjects for debate, speakers to open
in the affirmative and the negative, and arrange the programme
of the society's activities. They decide on all questions
arising within the society, and are generally responsible for
the drawing up of the code of rules.

This code of rules should state, under separate numbered
headings, the name of the club ; the officers ; their term of
office and method of election ; the regulations as to membership and subscriptions ; the times and days of meetings, both
committee and ordinary ; the way in which meetings are to
be conducted ; and miscellaneous rules governing the selection
of subjects for debate, the admission of visitors, etc.

At an ordinary meeting the chairman will first dispose of
the business of reading and approving the minutes, and any
private matters concerned with the working of the society ;
this he should do with as little delay as possible, as the majority
of those present will be anxious for the debate. Then, as
stated in the chapter on the Chairman's Duties, he will state
the subject, and call upon the openers in turn.

In open discussion it is usually the rule to allow each member
a certain time and one chance only ; although of course a
member may rise at any time " on a point of order." When
time is up, or no more debaters are forthcoming, the chairman
should call on the opener, or if there were two, upon both of

them in turn, to make a short reply to the criticisms advanced. The motion should then be put to the meeting and a vote taken by a show of hands. The result of the voting should be announced clearly by the chairman.

Members of any debating society should bear in mind that if it is worth while to speak at all on a subject it is worth while to acquire some knowledge beforehand. Above all, it should be remembered that contradition is not argument, and that every question has more than one aspect.

PART II

MODEL SPEECHES AND USEFUL MATERIAL FOR SPEAKERS

It will be noticed that the following models are almost all brief and simple in construction. They have been made so intentionally, being designed to serve as guides for first efforts. It will be found comparatively easy to lengthen one's speeches after a little practice and experience has been gained.

CHAPTER VII

GENERAL AND LOCAL ELECTIONEERING SPEECHES

(a) INTRODUCING A POLITICAL CANDIDATE

LADIES AND GENTLEMEN,—My first and chief duty as chairman this evening is to introduce to you Mr. —— as a candidate to represent the interests of this Borough in Parliament. A great many of you, possibly, know him better than I do. But, although my acquaintance with him has been of short duration, it has been sufficient to convince me that he is in every way an able exponent of the principle of the —— Party, and a man upon whom we may safely rely for the furtherance of the Party's aims. His election address should by this time have come into the hands of every elector in the Borough, and its straightforward and explicit nature will, I think, go a long way towards securing his success in the coming contest. As this meeting has been convened mainly to afford you the opportunity of hearing from Mr. —— himself his opinions upon the pressing questions of the day, I will trespass upon your time no more than is necessary to request you earnestly to give him a fair and patient hearing. Any questions you may desire to put he will be only too pleased to answer at the conclusion of his address. For my own part, I am satisfied that his address will be well worth your attention; and I may add that he has the promise of my support and vote. Ladies and gentlemen, Mr. —— will now address you.

(b) Supporting the Proposed Adoption of a Political Candidate

Mr. Chairman, Ladies and Gentlemen,—After hearing Mr. ——'s able exposition of his views, and, moreover, by reason of a knowledge of his character—gained during a long and intimate acquaintance—I have no hesitation in supporting the proposition that Mr. —— be adopted as the —— Party candidate to contest the coming election. For the benefit of those who, perhaps, are unacquainted with Mr. ——, I would like to give a brief account of the excellent work which he has done locally in connection with the —— and the —— during the last five years. The —— Organisation, to which he is now acting as general secretary, owes, I think I may say, practically the whole of its strength and efficiency to his untiring efforts, etc. . . . Those with whom Mr. —— comes in daily contact are unanimous in the opinion that his personality and energy are of inestimable value to any interests which it is his intention to further. That he has the interests of the electors of this Division at heart, I think should be plain to all; and that he intends to devote his whole attention to the matters of which he has just spoken is my firm conviction. As a citizen, Mr. —— is universally esteemed; and as a politician he has shown us that he possesses common sense coupled with fine ideals and worthy aspirations. Ladies and gentlemen, I have very great pleasure in supporting the proposal that we adopt Mr. —— as our candidate.

(c) Proposing a Candidate for a Municipal Election

Mr. Chairman, Ladies and Gentlemen,—It is with great pleasure and some pride that I rise to propose my friend Mr. —— as candidate for election to the —— Town Council. Those of you who know him as well as I do will have no hesitation in agreeing with me that he is the man we want. For the past few weeks he has been doing everything humanly possible to bring before his fellow-townsmen the principles and programme for which he stands. He is peculiarly adapted, in my opinion, to secure for the town, if he is elected, the consideration of those matters which have been, for reasons it is not my place to mention, so long neglected. Our Local Authority needs young men of energy and thoroughness more at the present time than ever before. It is impossible to disguise the fact that matters in this town are in a bad state—that is, as far as the interest of the workers, who are the bulk of the electors, is concerned. I would remind you of the . . . . . . These improvements, for which we have so long looked in vain, will never be secured without considerable pressure. The particular reforms most immediately desirable and attainable have been, and will be again, indicated by Mr. —— himself ; but I would emphasise to you this point, that however much we agree that they are desirable, we shall never obtain them unless we return as councillors men of definite purpose and perseverance. I unhesitatingly say that, from his past record, we know Mr. —— to be such a man ; and I therefore strongly recommend the electors to give him their undivided support.

(d) Opposing the Recommendation of a Candidate for Election

Mr. Chairman, Ladies and Gentlemen,—I have listened to Mr. ——'s address with considerable interest, and I am willing to pay him the tribute that he has stated his opinions honestly and well. You, Mr. Chairman, have advanced to us several good reasons demonstrating his suitability to represent us. Nevertheless, I feel it my duty to put before this meeting several points to which I think we should give further consideration before adopting him as our candidate. In the first place, Mr. ——, although he has touched upon the subject, has not dealt thoroughly with the question of . . . . . . His replies to various questions on the matter have been, to say the least, somewhat meagre. I will not say they were evasive ; but I suggest to you that this question of . . . . . . is of vital importance to us as electors, and is not one which can be satisfactorily dealt with by a policy such as Mr. —— has adopted in referring to it. He has expressed a general sort of agreement with what he terms " the Party's views " on the subject. To me it seems obvious that he has not devoted serious attention to it, and I protest that since the question is one that bulks large in our programme our duty is to select and elect for this constituency a candidate who thoroughly understands this matter, and who, moreover, intends to use his first and strongest efforts towards the furtherance of our aims in regard to it.

Concerning one or two other points, namely, ... and . . . . . ., it also appears that Mr. ——'s attitude is hardly representative of our own. We have at previous meetings passed resolutions strongly in favour of . . . . . . In regard to this, I respectfully suggest to you again that Mr. —— does not seem to take up a very definite position ; and what little he has said on the matter does not appear to me to be in entire agreement with our own opinions. I maintain, Mr. Chairman, that we need a candidate with very definite knowledge and intentions in regard to these matters ; Mr. —— will, I am sure, understand that what I say is said in no spirit of malice. But I honestly feel that much further consideration is necessary before we come to our final decision.

CHAPTER VIII

LOYAL AND PATRIOTIC SPEECHES AND TOASTS

1. LOYAL TOASTS

(Generally proposed by the chairman or president)

THE proposer is not required to make a speech. He simply says " Ladies and Gentlemen "—or " Gentlemen," according to the audience—and then gives the toast in its correct form. The forms of loyal toasts are issued officially with the approval of the King, changes being notified as they are made. The present loyal toasts are as follow :

(a) " The King."

(b) " The Queen, Queen Mary, Princess Elizabeth, the Duke of Edinburgh, Princess Margaret, and the other members of the Royal Family."

2. HIS MAJESTY'S FORCES

(a) *The Royal Navy*

(Proposed by the chairman)

Gentlemen,—I now have the honour to propose the toast of the " Silent Service "—the Royal Navy. It may well be silent, I think, since its deeds have ever spoken for themselves. From the days of the Armada to the Battle of the Atlantic it has provided one long unbroken list of successes, frequently won against heavy odds. Its task has been a hard one. Not only has it been responsible for the guarding of our long island coastline, but it has had to protect our vital sea routes and keep them open for shipping in all the great oceans of the world. As the senior service, it has a great tradition ; but at the same time it has always shown itself strikingly progressive. For many centuries naval warfare meant either ships against ships or ships against shore-batteries. In modern times ships have been attacked by two new weapons of deadly striking power—one from above and one from below. Together they constituted a challenge to the very existence of a navy— and, therefore, a challenge to the safety of our island home. Our Navy met this challenge and triumphed over it ; and if new weapons are levelled against it in the future, I am confident that it will find the answer to these as well.

Our ships are the finest in the world. But ships alone do not make a Navy. Of old we spoke of ships of oak and hearts of oak. Nowadays our ships are of steel ; and it is not too much to say that the staunchness of our sailors has evolved in a like manner with their ships. Nothing but iron courage and nerves of steel can stand the strain of naval warfare to-day. Our Navy is a force of which we can be more justly proud to-day than ever before. Therefore, gentlemen, I count on an enthusiastic response to my toast to Britain's sure shield—the Royal Navy !

(b) The Army

(Proposed by the chairman)

Gentlemen.—The superb achievements of the Navy and the spectacular triumphs of the R.A.F. have made our Army look like a sort of Cinderella of the Services. This is most unfair. Even in the new atomic age, warfare is still fundamentally territorial. The Second World War was fought with torpedoes and mines, bombs and rockets, and all manner of fiendish weapons for use in the sea and air ; but the final victory was won on land—by the British and Allied Armies.

The remarkable thing about our Army is that it exists, as it were, in spite of our natural inclinations. We are not a militarily minded nation. We do not glory in regimentation. To the average young Englishman putting on a uniform is at the best an unfortunate necessity. Military service is simply a duty, to be performed with a maximum of efficiency and a minimum of fuss. It is for this reason, I think, that our troops have gained the admiration of the world. Duties have taken them to many foreign countries, and their arrival has not always been greeted with enthusiasm. Yet, wherever they have been, and in whatever circumstances, they have quickly won the hearts of the civilian population. No other troops in the world have shown greater restraint and forbearance in the face of provocation. Nor is this the result of any over-harsh discipline—but, rather, it derives from that self-discipline that is characteristic of the British in and out of uniform. Experience has shown that our troops abroad are our best Ambassadors. They deserve all our admiration. Gentlemen—" the British Army ! "

(c) The Royal Air Force

(Proposed by the chairman)

Gentlemen,—Ours is a nation steeped in tradition, and nowhere is this more apparent than in the Armed Forces. Our Navy and our Army have each a long and glorious history. The history of our Air Force is much shorter—but not, I think, less glorious. It has shown that tradition does not depend only on great age—for, young as it is, the R.A.F. already has established its own distinctive tradition. (It has even established its own distinctive language, too !)

Events have played a large part in shaping the tradition of the R.A.F. While still a young Force, it was suddenly called upon to fight by itself one of the most critical battles in British history. The result was that epic which has rightly gone down in history under the name of " the Battle of Britain." Never has our Army or our Navy had to fight against greater odds than those that faced the R.A.F. in the dark days when it seemed that defeat could be averted only by a miracle. And so it was—by the miracle of the R.A.F. The cost was high, and none the less grievous because it was so freely paid. It would be unfair to the other gallant Services to suggest that the R.A.F. won the war by itself ; but I do not think any soldier or sailor will quarrel with me when I say that but for the deeds of the R.A.F. in the Battle of Britain, the war would not have been won at all.

The R.A.F. is still a young service, and its ways are suggestive of perennial youth. Behind its smooth and efficient organisation there seems to exist a spirit of youthful energy, of daring, even of impetuosity. This is part of its unique tradition. It is a very different tradition from that of the Navy, and again from that of the Army—not a better one, for traditions cannot be measured and compared ; but one peculiarly suited to the demands the Service is required to meet. This spirit was the inspiration of the greatest invention since the first power-driven aeroplane—an invention that was born in the very heart of the R.A.F.—the jet engine. Gentlemen, the toast is—" the Royal Air Force ! "

(d) " Our Noble Selves."

(A particular regiment, battery, or squadron. Proposed by the chairman)

Gentlemen,—I now rise to propose the toast of the evening, —— Squadron, the Royal ——. We have assembled here this evening with the primary intention of honouring, in our own way, the name of the old unit in which we have all, at one time or another, served. There can be few here who had earlier acquaintance with —— Squadron than myself. I saw many fresh faces come, remain for a while, and then depart for other spheres of activity. Several of those faces I am glad and proud to see here to-night. Some there were amongst my old friends and comrades who have since made the supreme sacrifice ; in making that sacrifice they have but borne their part in upholding and fashioning the glorious traditions which it has ever been our pride to maintain. But those who have passed out would be the last to wish us to be gloomy on an occasion such as this. What greater delight is there for old warriors than the fighting of old battles over again—with the aid of good wine and the fragrant weed ? Need I remind you of the strenuous days we passed at —— during the —— ? We earned there a reputation that made us the envy of our neighbours and rivals, the Royal ——. Need I speak of the great night we had when the news came through that ——'s great deed had earned him the soldier's most coveted reward ? No ; I see by your faces that the old memories glow within you yet. As a soldier is taught to do, I regard —— Squadron as the finest unit in His Majesty's Forces ; I am confident that its present members will never allow its glorious past to be forgotten ; I am confident they will add to its already great list of achievements ; and, finally, and above all, I am supremely confident that with enthusiasm and one accord you will drink with me to the continued honour of —— Squadron, the Royal ——'s !

(e) *A Typical Response to One of the Above*

Mr. Chairman and Gentlemen,—I feel I am quite unworthy of the honour that has been conferred upon me. I am far too junior a member of the Air Force to take upon my immature shoulders the task of replying, on behalf of the great Service of which I am so insignificant a part, to your enthusiastically expressed goodwill towards us. Perhaps my youthfulness was the cause of our worthy chairman's remarks on the youthful and impetuous spirit of the Force ! Be that as it may, I am far from denying the truth of his remarks ; but I would like to add my quota to what he also said in regard to the vast amount of humdrum routine work which it falls to our lot to perform. I know that we have a reputation for being rather a hare-brained, dare-devil crowd of young scamps. I even heard it said the other day that that same irresponsible spirit pervaded even that awe-inspiring institution called the Air Ministry, and that it was responsible for the reckless finance, etc., with which that body has been credited. But I would like to dispute the accusation. We are not so bad as we have been painted—not nearly so rash and impetuous as some would have you believe. Really, we are extremely cautious! For those who lack caution, I would remind you, do not last long in our profession! But, jesting on one side, I must say, gentlemen, that I feel greatly honoured by the way in which you have expressed your appreciation of the Service to which I belong ; and, as a humble member of that Service, I beg leave to return heartfelt thanks, on behalf of the Royal Air Force, for your generous expression of good feeling.

(f) " The Services " (a Short Form suitable for an Informal Gathering)

Mr. Chairman and Gentlemen,—Although to-night we have no formal toast-list, I feel that we ought not to let the evening pass without paying a tribute to the Services, many representatives of whom I know are present with us. There can scarcely exist to-day an individual who has not in the recent years had some more or less intimate connection with either the Army, the Navy, the Air Force, or one of the gallant Auxiliary Services. Therefore, I submit to you, gentlemen, as a pleasant duty, the toast of " His Majesty's Forces."

CHAPTER IX

SPEECHES FOR CLUB AND TRADE UNION OFFICIALS

(a) A CRICKET CLUB SECRETARY'S REPORT

MR. CHAIRMAN AND GENTLEMEN,—In preparing this report to place before you, I have endeavoured to be as brief as possible, and to arrange it in such a way that members—new members particularly—may obtain a comprehensive view of the club's development during the past year.

First, as to last season. Matches played numbered ——, of which we won ——, drew ——, and lost ——. On—— occasions visiting teams were entertained to lunch and tea. It was decided at last year's General Meeting to make this a rule, and I think it has received general approbation, and rendered the club popular.

Our membership during the year has increased very considerably—from —— to ——. This is very gratifying, and I attribute it mainly to our having obtained the new clubhouse and ground. There are some financial details in connection with the matter with which the treasurer will deal later.

With regard to the acquisition of the new club ground, I would remind you that the project was embarked upon not without considerable opposition, on grounds of finance and expediency, from a proportion of our old members. Enquiries as to alternative accommodation were accordingly made ; but the Committee's final decision was the right one, I think—for our present quarters are convenient and spacious, and have resulted, as I say, in raising considerably the status and popularity of the club.

Some new nets were acquired also towards the end of last season, were very well patronised, and will undoubtedly be required this season.

I must also refer to the three social events we held during the winter. They were each extremely successful, and I have been pressed by many members for a greater number in the future.

Coming now to my own work—the preliminaries for the coming season—I must first inform you that it has been decided to run two elevens. Matches to the number of —— for the first eleven, and —— for the second eleven are already arranged ; and " home " and " away " events have been fitted in so that the teams will have the use of our own ground alternately.

Finally, I wish to mention that many members have written urging the formation of a tennis club. I am inclined to favour the idea, since we have ample room for two or three courts ; and I will be glad to undertake the arrangements if the project meets with general approval.

(*b*) SPEECH BY THE SECRETARY OR OTHER OFFICIAL OF A
TRADE UNION IN SUBMITTING A QUESTION TO A GENERAL
MEETING

Mr. Chairman and Comrades,—This meeting has been called
in order that careful consideration may be given to the
question of the desirability or otherwise of . . . . . . The question
is one of peculiar difficulty ; it not only involves considerations
of finance and organisation, it involves questions of policy and
tactics, and—what is more important—the different political
views held by the individual members of our organisation.   In
our membership, as you know, we have men of varying shades
of political opinion.   Many hold their particular political views
very strongly ; so that in considering this matter, no sort of
general agreement can be hoped for unless some criterion is
applied which represents a point of view tenable by every
member whatever his political conviction.   The Committee
have directed me to suggest to you that the criterion we should
apply to a question of this kind is a very simple one—namely,
whether, considered in the light of an investment, the project
is one which is likely to yield a good return for the time, money,
and energy which we should have to put into it.   Our organisation exists mainly for the purpose of securing for its members
better conditions.   Will the project of . . . help us in that
object to a degree commensurate with its cost ?   That is the
question which I urge that each of you should put to himself.

I will now briefly set out the various arguments for and
against the project.   The case against is as follows :

First, ... ; second, ... ; etc.   The case in favour
is as follows : First, ... ; second, ... ; etc.

In conclusion, the Committee wish me to say that they are
themselves led by these latter considerations to recommend
the proposal as one which it will pay us to adopt.

(*c*) A TRADE UNION SECRETARY'S REPORT ON THE
YEAR'S WORK

Mr. Chairman and Gentlemen,—In making this report of
the things we have accomplished in our third year, I feel that,
despite undoubted failures in one or two directions, our
achievements have been such that we can afford to be really
proud of the year's work as a whole.   Perhaps the most

satisfactory information I have to give is that our membership has increased from —— at the beginning of the year to ——at the present time. We may congratulate ourselves on the result of our efforts in regard to . . . . . . At the outset things looked extremely black for us in that matter ; but, thanks to the energy and perseverance of Mr. —— and Mr. ——, after negotiations extending over a period of four months, a definite and fairly satisfactory settlement was reached. In the matter of . . . . . ., which I know is uppermost in your minds at present, a conclusion has not yet been reached ; but I think that I may say that so far our prospects in that direction may be considered good. Our other activities I will go over briefly in order that you may obtain a comprehensive view of the progress we have made.

We have held —— meetings, at which the attendances have steadily improved.

Of social gatherings we have held in all —— : they have been increasingly popular, and have proved on the whole profitable.

We have also . . . . . . , etc.

The general state of our finances you will have seen by the copies of the balance-sheet which have been circulated ; but there are one or two items therein about which I wish to say a few words in explanation. The expenditure on . . . . . . was necessitated by . . . . . . , etc.

In conclusion, gentlemen, I would point out that, although we have made gratifying progress, much still remains to be done. In the year that is now before us we must not relax effort—rather, we must increase it—if we are fully to justify ourselves and the principles by which we stand.

CHAPTER X

SOCIAL AND CONVIVIAL SPEECHES AND TOASTS

I. At Wedding, Birthday, and Coming of Age Parties

Toast to the Bride and Bridegroom

LADIES AND GENTLEMEN,—The making of speeches is an art of which I have little experience. But I feel impelled to call your attention to a little ceremony which I think we ought not to omit. Before we speed them on their journey, we must drink a bumper toast to the happy pair who have to-day embarked upon a great adventure. Of late we have heard much in regard to the matrimonial venture—we have been told that it is going out of fashion, that it is a lottery in which the prizes are all blanks, and much more to the same effect ; but I am inclined to think that the explanation of these vapourings is that they emanate from the bridegroom's unsuccessful rivals ! For there is no doubt in my mind that he has secured a prize, and that she, in her turn, has by no means drawn a blank. They agree with me, you see—observe it in their faces !

Hitherto I have been a contented bachelor ; but I must confess that to-day I envy my old friend the visions that I know he sees ; and I cannot say more than that I wish from the bottom of my heart that all his hopes may be fulfilled, and that he and his sweet bride will live long and happily to prove to me the error of my bachelor ways ! Ladies and gentlemen, let us drink to the long life, prosperity, and, above all, the happiness of the Bride and Groom!

Response by the Husband (with Toast to Bridesmaids)

Ladies and Gentlemen,—I thank you all for your kind thoughts. With so many warm friends, I fail to see why we should ever lack the happiness you wish us. For whatever may be in store for us, if we are to experience some of the trials and troubles that are mankind's common lot, I am sure that friendship such as yours will enable us to meet them with courage and surmount them with success.

I would like to say that I certainly intend to show my friend Mr. —— the error of his ways. So well do I know his worth, that I recommend him unreservedly to the single ladies present ; and so great is my esteem for the fair sex, that I recommend them even more unreservedly to his attention. And by the mutual interest I see already displayed, I am confident that before very long there will be interesting developments ! We have only to wait and see ! Meanwhile, in thanking you again, on behalf of my wife and myself, for your kindly good wishes, I wish to thank especially the ladies who have supported my wife in her trying ordeal, which, I secretly believe, she has enjoyed thoroughly, and I beg leave to give you a further toast. Ladies and gentlemen, " To the Bridesmaids." May they all officiate at one more wedding at least !

A Birthday Toast

Gentlemen,—For some reason or other several of you have conspired to force on me the duty of proposing the toast of the evening. My natural modesty would prevent me assuming such prominence of my own accord ; but since you wish it, and since the duty is one that is in itself a pleasure and an honour, I will endeavour to overcome my diffidence. I despair, however, of doing my subject justice. Of what use is it for me to attempt to enumerate the sterling qualities of him in whose honour this little gathering is held ? He is the very old friend of all of us, I think ; and for myself, I can say that I value his friendship as my most precious possession. My high opinion of him is shared by all with whom he has come in contact, both in public and in private life—of that I am sure. We have evidence of it in his popularity and prominence in all our local affairs. His generous hospitality is proverbial, and he is an ever-ready friend in need. No words of mine, as I say, can do him justice ; and in any case, his praise is superfluous at a gathering like this. So I will come to the point, and ask you to fill your glasses and drink Mr. ——'s very good health, wishing him " Many happy returns of the day ! "

At a Coming of Age

Ladies and Gentlemen,—It is now my pleasant duty to propose the health of the hero of the day. This is a great occasion for him—to-day he enters man's estate ; I think you will all agree with me that he is a worthy addition to our ranks.

But I do not intend to make a sententious oration. This is a convivial meeting, and we are here to enjoy ourselves ; and neither you nor I will do that if I continue this very stuttering utterance. My duty is simply to ask you to toast

our friend in the good old-fashioned way. So, gentlemen, fill
up and drink up to our good friend Mr. ——.

" For he's a jolly good fellow ! "

2. AT ATHLETIC AND SPORTS CLUB MEETINGS

A Toast to " Our Opponents "

(Proposed by the captain of one of the teams at a football
match dinner)

Gentlemen,—You have greatly honoured me in selecting me
to act as your chairman to-night, and I take this early opportunity of discharging what is perhaps the most pleasant of the
duties which devolve upon my office—that is, the proposal of
a toast to our opponents. The —— team have to-day given
us a lesson in the way football should be played ; but the
game, although it went against us, was, nevertheless, enjoyable—to me, at any rate. I am not, of course, going to bore
you with excuses for our failure. We did our best, every man
of us ; but our adversaries, on this occasion, we must admit,
did better. Every member of my team will agree with me
that the wonderful defence which we encountered is deserving
of the highest compliment. Those sturdy backs, —— and
——, if they will permit me to say so, played a wonderfully
skilful, hard, and clean game, and I, for one, shall remember
not to underestimate their prowess at our next meeting ! At
that next meeting, of course, our positions will be reversed—I
have no doubt of it ! I should be guilty of disloyalty if I
thought otherwise ! But I acknowledge that our task will be
no easy one, and I look forward with particular pleasure to
what I am sure will be one of the best games of the season.
To-day we have enjoyed a great match ; after all, victory or
defeat matters little to the true lover of the national game.
We would sooner lose a hard game, such as to-day's, than win
an easy one—you will all agree with that, I know. The play's
the thing, gentlemen ! No team can expect always to win ;
but next time you shall see things ! Meanwhile, let us do
honour where honour is due. Gentlemen, " Our Worthy
Opponents."

Response to the Above

Mr. Chairman and Gentlemen,—On behalf of my fellow-players, I rise to thank you most heartily for the high tribute you have paid us ; but, Mr. Chairman, I must protest that you have been too complimentary.   Our success was gratifying to us, naturally ; but we must not forget that Dame Fortune helped us in no little degree. Had she been more impartial with her favours—well, the issue might have been very different.

Personally, I can say that the " wonderful defence " referred to was hard put to it on several occasions this afternoon.   If we made a good show, it was because a formidable attack demanded of us our very best.   I, in my turn, can assure you that I have resolved to bear well in mind that splendid short-passing combination which worried me more than a little to-day ! And there is a left wing which I have privately decided will require special attention at our next meeting !

With all our chairman has said I am in thorough agreement : a fast, hard game is the thing we look for and enjoy, no matter what the result.   Football—the playing of it, I mean—brings out all that is best in a man. The selfish individualist has no place in the game ; a man must play for his team, and in the doing so he learns self-denial as well as self-reliance.   What is more, he learns to respect an honourable opponent, and to accept defeat generously and without loss of confidence, as you have shown us.

In conclusion, gentlemen, I must again thank you for the hearty reception and splendid game you have given us.

At a Boating-Club Dinner

Gentlemen,—We are now coming towards the close of a sporting day and a jolly evening, and my final duty as chairman is to call on you for one last toast, to the success of our Club.   Other speakers have spoken of the stirring events of the day—our gains, our losses, and our hopes and intentions in regard to the future.   I am afraid, however, that one worthy individual has not received his due meed of praise. I refer to the Clerk of the Weather.   Without his kind assistance our regatta could scarcely have been such a dazzling success.

D

I am afraid that time will not permit me to say all that is in my mind ; but, before closing, I would like to add my quota to what the last speaker has said in praise of our worthy host. I have been behind the scenes, and I know that he has strained every effort to make our evening a complete and noteworthy success. His excellent fare and splendid arrangements have, I know, been thoroughly appreciated ; but all good things must have an end. Therefore, gentlemen, the last toast, please—and bumpers ; " Success to the —— Rowing Club ! "

The Health of the Gold Medallist

(At a Golf Club Dinner)

Mr. Chairman, Ladies and Gentlemen,—On occasions like this, and in proposing a toast that is necessarily a pleasurable duty, it may be permitted for one to be momentarily autobiographical. I well remember, with somewhat mixed emotions, how, after cooling my heels in a queue at the first tee, I addressed the ball in my first match. I had been favoured in my initial practices with more than the usual luck that falls to the lot of the novice. But at the first tee everything was different. Doubtless many of you have experienced that awful oozing away of the feeling of certitude and self-assurance with which a round is started. I experienced it to the full on that occasion ; and the memory of that awful ordeal of frantic attempts to reach the first green will never leave me.

Although since then I have made some little progress in " the royal and ancient game "—which satisfies me more perhaps than the partners who are unfortunate enough to share my rounds—I have, if possible, an even more profound admiration nowadays for the man who plays " straight and long " than I had in the far-off days of my novitiate.

" Lies " in golf are proverbially " hard." But lying is easy. You will not need reminding of this. Your own accounts of a match, of course, never vary in the slightest degree from the cold bare facts ! But your neighbour's account of *his* match is one that you generally feel is handled with a somewhat careless regard for the truth !

When, however, one is hearing the account of a round played by a third person, one is reasonably sure that the performance will not suffer from magnification. And it was my good fortune recently to witness the performance of our good friend ——, when, by his masterful play and wonderful resource in extricating himself from difficulties, he succeeded not only in winning the club's gold medal, but in putting up a record that will always be the admiration of his fellow-members, and an incentive to them to try to follow in his wake. And the impression I received was that it was magic—not golf such as we play !

It is unnecessary for me to refer to the fine sportsmanlike character of our friend—we all know him too well. I feel that I shall have everyone present with me when I express the wish that our guest's form may never be below that of his medal round, and that our best efforts will be devoted to getting individually as near to it as we can. Gentlemen, " The Winner of the Gold Medal ! "

3. MISCELLANEOUS

The Health of the Vicar

(Proposed at a County Function)

Mr. Chairman, Ladies and Gentlemen,—There can be no toast more welcome than that which I am now about to propose, namely, the health of our esteemed Vicar. For myself, I revere him as a trusty friend no less than as an able minister of religion ; and I am sure that sentiment will be echoed by every one of his parishioners. The Vicar, as you are doubtless aware, is one of those to whom the present success of this fuction is largely due, and his creditable efforts in this connection are merely the outcome of his ever-present and sincere interest in the welfare of our county. In proof of that statement I need only remind you of the fact that there is scarcely an institution within our borders here of which our Vicar is not an important pillar. To him proposals for the formation of football and cricket clubs and the holding of entertainments, etc., are invariably first submitted, with positive assurance of practical sympathy and help. So kind is his personality that

he is a thrice welcome guest in all our homes—into which he
ever brings an atmosphere of clear Christian optimism which
never fails to help us both spiritually and materially.   Of the
Vicar's work in discharging the duties of his holy office I need
not speak—only those of us who, in times of sorrow, have
experienced his tender ministrations can fully appreciate how
great is his understanding.   He is, alike in prosperity and
adversity, to one and all of us, a real " guide, philosopher, and
friend " ; and in giving you this toast, I regret only that I am
unable to do full justice to its subject.   Ladies and gentlemen,
" Our good Vicar ! "

A Toast to " The Press "

Mr. Chairman and Gentlemen,—Of late the Press has been
the recipient of much criticism of a sort far removed from
kindly.   Street-corner orators are for ever denouncing us for
taking our opinions direct from newspapers, and are for ever
accusing the " Fourth Estate " of furthering the evil designs
of some tyrant or other.   I suppose that a paper must have
its policy—and I do not propose to raise any controversy on
such an occasion as this.   But it occurs to me that as " a
nation gets the Government is deserves " so does it get the
Press that it deserves.   In my humble opinion, the chief
concern of an editor or newspaper proprietor is to sell his paper,
and with that end in view it seems to me that of necessity he
supplies the public with what it wants.   Granting that our
Press has its faults, and is not, for excellent reasons, quite so
free and outspoken as some of us would like, at least we must
admit that it compares extremely favourably with that of
other countries. The Press of this country, considering all
things, is an institution of which we may be proud.   To all
who quarrel with it I would say that its improvement rests
with themselves.   It cannot be denied that the Press is a
really useful factor in the daily life and in the education of the
nation.   I maintain that the Press of Britain is at least as
good as, if not better than, we deserve, and I call upon you to
drink to it, and to Mr. ——, who is, I believe, its representative
here to-night.

Response to Foregoing, by a Member of the Staff of a Paper

Mr. Chairman and Gentlemen,—As a Pressman I am used to having showered upon my head recriminations of the nature referred to by Mr. ——. I had intended to say something in defence, but Mr. —— has said it for me. I can, from my professional capacity, bear witness to the truth of his remarks. I can assure you that an editor's sole endeavour is to provide the public with what it wants—that is, as far as is possible. Speaking personally, and on behalf of my brethren of the pen, I may say that in *our* opinion this country has a Press a great deal better than it deserves ! These things are bound to be largely a matter of opinion ; but from the very kind sentiments that have just been expressed, I am convinced that our efforts are not by any means unappreciated ; and I beg of you to accept from me, in the absence of a fitter representative, the assurance that the Press returns your goodwill most heartily.

A Toast to One of the Dominions

Gentlemen,—The days of Imperial jingoism are over, and I do not think any of us regret their passing. The old conception of the British Empire has given way to the much finer ideal of the British Commonwealth of Nations. The ties that now bind us together are less obvious but far stronger than before, because they rest on sounder foundations. We have much to be proud of in the achievements of the old Empire ; but our greatest pride must surely lie in the way it has developed into the Commonwealth as it is to-day. It is an example to the world of how free, democratic peoples, separated from one another by many thousands of miles, can live together in a voluntary association based on goodwill and mutual help. The solidarity of that association has twice been sorely tested during this century, and on each occasion it has gained from the ordeal. At the beginning of the Second World War, I remember, we from the Old Country used to call ourselves " British troops," and we were at first puzzled when an official directive assigned us the description of "United Kingdom troops." In our thoughtless vanity it had not occurred to us that other people of the Commonwealth also took a pride in being called British !

The achievements of Australia's fighting men need no fresh recital from me now. They are too well known, and have taken an honoured place in history. Little good comes out of the evils of war ; but those of us who were privileged to serve alongside Australian troops gained a new experience in comradeship that will never be forgotten. I do not need to remind you how that spirit continued in the happier days of peace. When this country entered the long struggle for recovery, it was the Australians who were the first to give us the help we so badly needed. It was the Australians who sent us food—not out of any surplus of their own, but by pure self-denial. When our food was rationed through force of necessity, the Australians rationed themselves simply in order to help us. We shall never forget this.

The British are often accused of paying too much attention to sport. We in the Old Country acknowledge the fault, and I think I am right in saying that the Australians also plead guilty to the charge. If the Test Matches mean as much to them as they do to us, then they are very important events indeed. Their true significance goes far beyond the score-board. To both of us sport means not only playing a game, but sportsmanship and fair play. The Australians excel at many sports beside cricket ; but what arouses our admiration most is their supreme excellence in the quality of sportsmanship. Gentlemen,—I give you " The Commonwealth of Australia—may it ever prosper ! "

A Toast to " The School "

(At an Old Boys' Reunion)

Gentlemen,—The Old School Tie has been the subject of so many music-hall jokes that one might expect it to have been laughed out of existence. Yet there seems to be plenty of evidence to the contrary here to-night ; and the fact that it has survived so much ridicule surely proves that it is by no means a meaningless symbol. Most loyalties are difficult to explain, and loyalty to the School is no exception. Old Boys' Associations differ from other societies in one important respect : their members are not proposed and elected, and indeed have little say in the matter of qualification for membership. The only thing that we have in common, on the face of it, is that our respective parents happened to send us to the same educational establishment ; and one might ask what bond can exist among us. The answer is not far to seek. As boys we were drawn together in comradeship not because we liked the look of each other's faces—I am sure you will agree with me on this point—but through loyalty to a common ideal. The strength of that ideal lies in the fact, of which we have abundant evidence here now, that it continues to hold us together after the end of our communal life. It is not easy to express its source of inspiration. It has nothing to do with the School's scholastic or sporting achievements ; it does not derive from the School buildings or grounds ; it does not even come from the headmaster and the teaching staff—saving their presence—although without their good influence it could hardly survive. It is simply one of those imponderables, and can only be defined as the Spirit of the School—a spirit compounded of honour, teamwork, comradeship and all that is best in communal life. Gentlemen,—" The School ! "

A Presentation to a Member of the Staff on Retirement

Ladies and Gentlemen,—At an occasion such as this our feelings are bound to be mixed. Mr. Smith is leaving us to-day, after thirty years' continuous service with the firm, to enjoy a well-deserved retirement. He takes with him our earnest wishes for his continued health and happiness for many years to come. No one would begrudge Mr. Smith the rest he has earned after his years of hard and selfless work. Yet we cannot pretend that we are happy to see him leave us. I do not want to say much about his value to the firm, because this is a matter of which we shall be reminded, often painfully, for a long time to come. No one is indispensable, but there are some people it is very difficult to do without, as I fear we are shortly going to discover. We are going to miss our Production Manager—but much more are we going to miss Mr. Smith the man.

As is natural in an organisation of this kind, our respective relationships with Mr. Smith have varied a good deal. To some he has been " one of the bosses," to be addressed as

" Sir." Others have known him just as " Mr. Smith." To others, again, he has been simply " Smith " ; and to a few intimate colleagues he has been plain " Jack." But his attitude to us has never reflected these differences. He has treated us all with the same unfailing courtesy and good humour. He has never been one to smile at the Directors and scowl at the junior clerks—indeed, from my personal experience he has inclined rather to smiling at the juniors and scowling at the Directors ! By his cheerfulness and natural friendliness Mr. Smith has earned the respect of every one of us, and it is with a sense of real loss that we see him go. On behalf of the staff, I have the great pleasure to present Mr. Smith with this small token of our esteem and affection.

Response to the Above

Ladies and Gentlemen,—My feelings at this moment are too deep for me to express adequately my gratitude for your generous gift and especially for the kind wishes that accompany it. It is difficult for me to realise that I am to-day leaving this firm where I have worked for so many years. I shall, I think, be quite happy without my work—and, in spite of Mr. Jones's kind words, I have not the slightest doubt that the work will get along very well without me. I was going to say that I have been only a cog in the machine, but I think a happier and more accurate description would be a member of a team. The small part I have played in this team has been made easy for me by the loyal co-operation I have always received from every other member. And it is the thought of leaving this team that makes parting so difficult for me. If I have smiled, it is because I have been happy here. If I have scowled—I had no right to. Now my innings has come to an end, but I shall watch the future achievements of the team from my seat in the pavilion. You have given me a splendid souvenir to take with me, which, I think, is out of all proportion to the modest contribution of my service. I shall always prize this gift and what it stands for. My thanks are halting, I know, but they are sincere. Sometimes feelings are too strong for words. Thank you again, all of you—good luck and good-bye !

A Chairman's Opening Remarks at a Smoking Concert

Gentlemen,—I am glad that my official position as chairman this evening does not carry with it very onerous duties. I notice these little functions of ours are growing in popularity, and I judge that their popularity is due to the excellence of the entertainment provided. At any rate, I am quite certain that it is not to hear a verbose chairman that you come ; so I will be brief. We have a long and varied programme before us—music, vocal and instrumental, and a morsel of dramatic art—for all of which we are indebted to Mr. —— and Mr. ——, in whose hands have been all the arrangements. I must remind you of our custom in regard to choruses, and—without offence, I hope—drop you the hint to order your refreshments *between* the items. That is all I need say, I think. We are " all assembled, so let the revels commence." I call upon Mr. —— for the opening item on our programme, which is . . . . . .

Space precludes more examples being given at full length ; but if the reader will observe in the foregoing the general method of construction, and of opening and concluding, he should be able without difficulty to make use of the following outlines :

" *The Firm* " (*at a House Dinner*).—Knowledge of the firm extending over many years of service. Their personal as well as business relations with us. Many acts of kindness. Bestowing the encouraging word of praise. The co-operation of the employer and employed. Willing service rather than grudging toil. Our firm an outstanding example of the value of these principles. Our excellent relations in the past may continue in the future.

" *The Employees.*"—A toast second only in importance to " the Firm." The head is of no value without limbs, and vice versa. The secret of business success is straightforward and considerate treatment of employees. What is expected in return. Intelligent service a mutual benefit. Thanking you for your past loyalty and efficiency. The firm conscious of your value, and sincerely grateful.

Response to Above.—All of us appreciate the kindness of to-day and of the past. These annual events are always appreciated. They show the excellent footing on which we stand towards each other. Glad to know that our efforts are valued. Promise as faithful service in the future. Thanking the firm again for their kindness.

" *The Ladies*."—An important toast that should not have been left till so late. My inability to do them justice. The vexed question of the equality of the sexes. Their splendid work in two wars. Their equality, if not superiority, proved, and a better understanding in sight. A pulling together towards better things. " Sweethearts and Wives," for whom all great deeds are accomplished !

"*Absent Friends*."—A simple toast with a wealth of meaning. " The old folks at home." The adventurers in other lands. Good friends scattered across the world.. Hands across the sea. Present with us in the spirit. A silent toast.

" *The Nursing Services*."—Service in its highest form. Hard work and little material reward. The spirit of the service. Heroines of peace and war : Florence Nightingale, the " Lady with the Lamp "—the tradition carried on. Good temper and kindness even to the most ungrateful patients. Edith Cavell—courage and devotion to duty in the highest sense of the words. Hundreds of other heroines who have remained anonymous. How little we appreciate the nursing services.

" *The Police Force*."—A toast commendable to all *law-abiding* citizens. Our dependence upon the man in blue. If you want to know the time, the way, or to cross the road. Duty continuously and quietly done. " A policeman's lot is not a happy one "—not without its risks. Must not, of course, mention the subject of *cooks !* Appreciation not too often shown, so now's the time.

" *Success to the* —— *Angling Club*."—I am an unfortunate fish, landed with the task I am unfitted for. Not fishing for compliments. Speech-making not in my *line*. To-day's sport—which will never decrease in the telling ! The immortal Izaak Walton. A modern opinion of fishing; " Perpetual expectation, continual disappointment." Angling produces the philosopher—develops the virtue of patience. Our club and its long record. Our good fellowship. Past occasions such as this. A sport and a club that will never decline !

" *The prosperity of the —— Golf Club.*"—Really a toast to " Our Noble Selves "—expect therefore hearty support—but includes " The Royal and Ancient." No worthier subject. The ideal relaxation, whether a *plus* man or not. Combines skill and reasonable open-air exercise. Promotes good-fellowship. The sport increasing in devotees. Number of new clubs. Golf and life. Golf maxims—" Keep your eye on the ball," " Don't press," " Hard and straight "—equally applicable to life. Golf language—sometimes really necessary ! Drink to still greater popularity of the game, still further prosperity to the club, and the health of our hard-working secretary.

At a Cycling Club Meeting.—Our excellent ride, this excellent repast, the enjoyable return journey before us. Cycling a fine inexpensive recreation. The joys of the open air. The poor man's ever-ready horse. Cycling in the past an eccentric's pastime. The old quaint cycling costumes—especially the ladies ! Famous cycling journeys—John Foster Fraser's " Round the World on a Wheel," etc. Interesting journeys nearer home. Local places of interest. Prosperity to our club—" A long run and no punctures."

" *The Women's Services.*"—A relatively new toast. It used to be an exclusively male function to serve one's country, but in this, as in every other sphere of modern life, we have had to ask the ladies to help us out. Origin of the Women's Services—pioneer work in First World War. In Second World War, fought in the front line in the Battle of Britain. Heroic work of mixed A.A. Batteries. Called " Auxiliaries," but soldiers forced to acknowledge them as comrades, sharing duties and dangers. After First World War, were stood down ; but now the nation has realised that even in peacetime we cannot do without them. Salute to the gallant women of the Services !

SOME USEFUL QUOTATIONS AND APHORISMS

" Blessed is the man who, having nothing to say, abstains from giving us wordy evidence of the fact."—GEORGE ELIOT.

" In general those who have nothing to say contrive to spend the longest time in doing it."—J. R. LOWELL.

" I am no orator, as Brutus is ;
But, as you know me all, a plain blunt man."
SHAKESPEARE, Julius Cæsar

" I would be loath to cast away my speech, for beside that it is excellently well penn'd, I have taken great pains to con it."—SHAKESPEARE, Viola in Twelfth Night.

" Do you want people to speak well of you ?   Then do not speak at all yourself."—PASCAL.

" As a vessel is known by the sound, whether it be cracked or not ; so men are proved, by their speeches, whether they be wise or foolish."—DEMOSTHENES.

" Be sure to leave other men their turns to speak."—FRANCIS BACON.

" Let him now speak, or else hereafter for ever hold his peace."—BOOK OF COMMON PRAYER (Solemnisation of Matrimony).

" This England never did, nor never shall,
Lie at the proud foot of a conqueror."
SHAKESPEARE, King John.

" He who loves not his country can love nothing."—BYRON.

" A faithful friend is the medicine of life."—APOCHRYPHA.

" They are rich who have true friends."—THOMAS FULLER.

" Advice to persons about to marry—Don't."—PUNCH'S ALMANACK.

" No woman should marry a teetotaller, or a man who does not smoke."—R. L. STEVENSON.

" Every woman should marry—and no man."—BENJAMIN DISRAELI.

" Is not marriage an open question, when it is alleged, from the beginning of the world, that such as are in the institution wish to get out, and such as are out wish to get in ? "—EMERSON.

" Man has his will : but woman has her way."—O. W. HOLMES.

" Woman will be the last thing civilised by man."—MEREDITH.

" I don't care where the water goes if it doesn't get into the wine."—G. K. CHESTERTON.

> " Man, being reasonable, must get drunk ;
> The best of life is but intoxication."
>
> BYRON

" ' It wasn't the wine,' murmured Mr. Snodgrass in a broken voice, ' it was the salmon.' "—DICKENS, *Pickwick Papers*.

" A fishing-rod is a stick with a hook at one end and a fool at the other."—DR. JOHNSON.

" Absent in body, but present in spirit."—I CORINTHIANS.

" A woman is only a woman, but a good cigar is a smoke."—KIPLING.

FOULSHAM'S POCKET LIBRARY

1. HOW TO TALK CORRECTLY.   By Professor Duncan
4. WILD FLOWERS : How and Where to Find Them.
   By Wm. Platt
5. CORRECT CONDUCT : Perfect Etiquette for All.
   By M. Woodman
6. HOW TO DRIVE A CAR EFFICIENTLY.
   By a Driving Instructor
7. HOW TO WRITE CORRECTLY.   By Professor Duncan
11. COBBETT'S EASY GRAMMAR.   Makes Study a Pleasure.
12. THE RAMBLER'S POCKET GUIDE to Life and Growth
   by the Wayside.   By S. C. Johnson, M.A.
14. 100 VARIETIES OF SANDWICHES.   By Mary Woodman
15. HOW TO CALCULATE QUICKLY AND CORRECTLY.
16. CORRECT BOOK-KEEPING.   By J. H. Burton, A.S.A.A.
17. BILLIARDS : How to Play and Win.   By Melbourne Inman
20. EVERYBODY'S READY RECKONER : $\frac{1}{16}$d. to 19s. 6d.
23. HOME-MADE WINES.   By Mary Woodman
28. PUBLIC SPEAKING.   By Professor Duncan
31. 100 COCKTAILS : How to Mix Them.   By "Bernard"
36. HOW TO CONDUCT MEETINGS.   Procedures fully explained.
39a. MODERN BUSINESS LETTER WRITING.   By S. C. Johnson
41. CONSTRUCTIVE THINKING.   By H. Ernest Hunt
43. YOUR NERVES : How to Control Them.   By Dr. J. B——
44. HOW TO SPELL CORRECTLY.   By Professor Duncan
50. HOW TO TRAIN THE MEMORY.   By H. Ernest Hunt
52. EVERYBODY'S VEGETARIAN COOKERY BOOK.
   By E. Forster
59. CORRECT PUNCTUATION: Effective Sentence Construction.
   By Max Crombie
62. SIXTY BEST HUMOROUS RECITATIONS.
63. VEGETABLE AND FRUIT GROWING.   By Rosslyn Mannering
64. THE GARDENER'S WEEKLY GUIDE.   By Rosslyn Mannering

Obtainable from all Booksellers

W. FOULSHAM & CO. LTD.
20 & 21 Red Lion Court, Fleet St., London, E.C.4.

Foulsham's Wireless Guides

Each Vol. 6¼ x 4 *ins.*   *Fully Illustrated.*   *Bound Stiff Cover*

1. WIRELESS REALLY EXPLAINED

By P. J. RISDON. Revised and up-to-date.

Explains everything in an easy-to-understand manner, including the various Symbols used in modern Circuit Diagrams.

2. SHORT WAVE RADIO RECEPTION

By W. OLIVER

The future of Broadcasting lies in the wavelengths below 100 metres. This up-to-date handbook gives much practical information concerning this important development in Wireless. It includes Circuit Diagrams and guidance for making a Short-Wave Receiver, and for adapting an ordinary set.

4. WIRELESS QUESTIONS AND ANSWERS

By P. J. RISDON

This volume explains, in an interesting question and answer form, the why and wherefore of many things in Broadcasting and Television.

5. MAKING & REPAIRING RADIO SETS

By W. OLIVER

How to do your own repairs. How to make your own Battery or Mains Set. How to charge accumulators at home. A handy reference book.

Of all Booksellers

LONDON: W. FOULSHAM & CO., LTD.

20 & 21 Red Lion Court, Fleet Street, E.C.4

2/-
net

2/-
net

COLOURFUL
BONNIE BOOKS
for
YOUNG CHILDREN

THESE ARE THE FIRST SIXTEEN TITLES

1. SKY HIGH
2. OLD MACDONALD'S FARM
3. THROUGHOUT THE DAY
4. FARM ANIMALS
5. MAKE BELIEVE
6. FAVOURITE NURSERY RHYMES
7. PETER GETS HIS WISH
8. THE ELEPHANT'S DILEMMA

9. A IS FOR APPLE
10. PANCHO THE DONKEY
11. SLAPPY
12. McDUFF
13. MOTHER GOOSE RHYMES
14. BOBBIE HAD A SIXPENCE
15. ANIMALS ON AND NEAR THE FARM
16. THE LITTLE TOWN ON THE HILL

Four beautiful colours on every page. Strongly
bound in stout boards with a four-colour high-
gloss cover. Size $8\frac{1}{4} \times 6\frac{1}{4}$ in.

*Obtainable from all Booksellers 2s. net each or
Post Free 2s. 3d. each from the Publishers*

W. FOULSHAM & CO. LTD.
(Dept. S)

20 & 21 RED LION COURT, FLEET STREET,
LONDON, E.C.4